The Sioux

by Petra Press

Content Adviser: Professor Sherry L. Field,
Department of Social Science Education, College of Education,
The University of Georgia

Reading Adviser: Dr. Linda D. Labbo,
Department of Reading Education, College of Education,
The University of Georgia

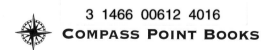

COMPASS POINT BOOKS

Minneapolis, Minnesota

FIRST REPORTS

Compass Point Books
3722 West 50th Street, #115
Minneapolis, MN 55410

Visit Compass Point Books on the Internet at *www.compasspointbooks.com* or e-mail your request
to *custserv@compasspointbooks.com*

Photographs ©: Colorado Historical Society, cover; Marilyn "Angel" Wynn, 4, 11, 12, 13, 14, 15
(top and bottom), 30, 32, 37, 42; Sharon Gerig/Tom Stack and Associates, 5; XNR Productions,
Inc., 6; Unicorn Stock Photos/Robert E. Barber, 7; Minnesota Historical Society, 8; Stock
Montage, 9, 28; The Newberry Library/Stock Montage, 10, 27, 34; David F. Clobes, 16, 17, 41;
Archive Photos, 18, 31; Library of Congress, 19, 36; Stock Montage, 20; Hulton Getty/Archive
Photos, 21, 23, 24, 25; Jeff J. Daly/Visuals Unlimited, 22; Denver Public Library, Western History
Collection, 26, 35, 38; Unicorn Stock Photos/Jean Higgins; Brian Parker/Tom Stack and
Associates, 33; John Shaw/Tom Stack and Associates, 40.

Editors: E. Russell Primm, Emily J. Dolbear, and Alice K. Flanagan
Photo Researcher: Svetlana Zhurkina
Photo Selector: Alice K. Flanagan
Designer: Bradfordesign, Inc.

Library of Congress Cataloging-in-Publication Data
Press, Petra.
    The Sioux / by Petra Press.
        p. cm. — (First reports)
    Includes bibliographical references and index.
    ISBN 0-7565-0084-2
    1. Dakota Indians—History—Juvenile literature. 2. Dakota Indians—Social life and customs—
Juvenile literature. I. Title. II. Series.
E99.D1 P86 2001
978'0049752—dc21   00-011284

Table of Contents

The Great Sioux Nation

▲ *A Sioux man in traditional clothing*

South Dakota is the home of the Sioux (pronounced SOO). The Sioux were once a large **nation**. Today, there are three main groups or divisions of Sioux. These groups are the Dakota, the Nakota, and the Lakota. Each group has its own language.

▲ *The Sioux lived in the Eastern Woodlands along Lake Superior.*

Long ago, the Sioux lived in the Eastern Woodlands along Lake Superior. They did not get along with their neighbors—the Ojibwa, or Chippewa. Slowly, the Ojibwa drove the Sioux away.

The Dakota (Eastern or Santee Sioux) moved near lakes in western and southern Minnesota. The Nakota

CANADA

Alberta   Saskatchewan   Lake Winnipegosis   Lake Winnipeg   Ontario

Lake Manitoba   Lake of the Woods   Lake Nipigon

Manitoba

Missouri

Montana   North Dakota   Minnesota   Lake Superior   Mich.

Battle of Little Bighorn, June 1876

Idaho   South Dakota   Wisconsin   Lake Michigan

Wyoming   Battle of Wounded Knee, 1890

Fort Laramie   North Platte   Nebraska   Iowa   Illinois

Great Salt Lake

UNITED STATES   Missouri   Mississippi

Utah   Colorado   Kansas

Colorado   Arkansas   Missouri

Arizona   New Mexico

	Sioux lands at time of European contact
	Present-day Sioux Reservations
✹	Battle site
⌂	Fort

0   100   200 miles
0   100   200 kilometers

▲ The original homelands of the Sioux and their present homes.

▲ *The Lakota Sioux moved as far west as the Teton Mountains in Wyoming.*

(Middle or Yankton Sioux) settled on the prairies east of the Missouri River. And the Lakota (Western or Teton Sioux) settled on the **Great Plains** between the Missouri River and the Teton Mountains.

From the Woodlands to the Plains

▲ *The Dakota fished from canoes.*

The Dakota lived much like other Eastern **Woodland people**. The women planted corn, squash, and beans in fields outside the village. They gathered wild rice and other plants. The men speared fish from canoes. They also hunted bear, deer, moose, rabbits, and wild turkeys.

The Lakota were mainly hunters. They lived on the Great Plains. Following the buffalo herds, they moved often. People who move often are called **nomads**.

▲ *The Lakota moved with the buffalo herds.*

The Lakota lived in cone-shaped tents called tepees. The tepees were made of buffalo skin stretched between wooden poles. Tepees made fine houses for people on the move. They could be carried easily from place to place. And they were warm in winter and cool in summer.

The Nakota lived on the prairies between the Lakota and the Dakota. They shared some traditions. Buffalo were important to the Nakota way of life, as they were to the Lakota.

▲ *The Nakota lived on the prairie, much like the Lakota.*

Hunting the Buffalo

The Sioux always traveled in groups called **bands**.
They followed the buffalo and other wild animals.

Before the Sioux had horses, they hunted buffalo

▲ *Before the arrival of horses, the Sioux hid beneath animal skin and hunted on foot.*

on foot. A band of hunters would surround a herd of buffalo near a cliff. Then they would chase the animals off the cliff to their death.

▲ *The Sioux hunted buffalo by driving them off cliffs.*

Almost everything the Sioux needed for their daily lives came from the buffalo. After a buffalo was killed, every part of its body was used. Nothing was wasted.

Women dried the meat and stored it for the future. They **tanned** the skins. Then they sewed the skins together to make moccasins, robes, and other

▲ Robes were just one of many things the Sioux made from buffalo.

warm clothing. From buffalo bones they carved toys, tools, and sewing needles. Even the buffalo droppings were used as fuel in campfires.

To the Sioux, the buffalo was a **sacred** animal. They said a prayer before killing the buffalo.

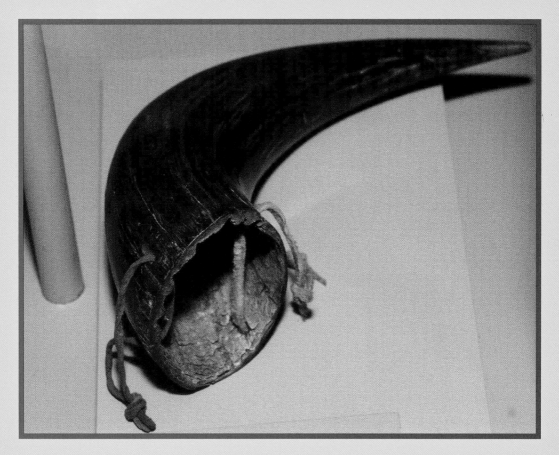

▲ *A cup carved from buffalo horn*

A Prayerful People

The Sioux believed in one god. They called him Wakantanka (the Great Spirit). They prayed often to Wakantanka and sang songs to him. They smoked special pipes to help their prayers be heard. They held special ceremonies to

▲ *The Vision Quest ceremony honors the Sioux god.*

bring them success in hunting and war.

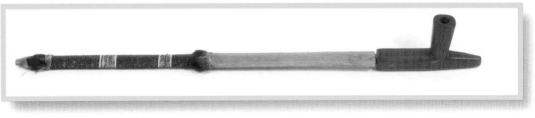

▲ *A ceremonial peace pipe*

The Sioux also had ceremonies to protect them from danger and sickness. The buffalo and the bear had special meaning for the Sioux. They honored the spirits of those animals.

Each summer, the Sioux held a Sun Dance. At this time, tribes came together to share news and to trade. They held contests to show their bravery. Many **fasted** and prayed to the Great Spirit for special favors. In return, they cut their bodies to prove their bravery as they danced beneath the hot sun.

Today, the Sun Dance still takes place. It is a sacred time for the Sioux.

▲ *A traditional dance performed in Rosebud, South Dakota*

▲ *A young girl performs at a celebration.*

The Importance of Family

▲ *Family is central to the Sioux.*

The Sioux were proud of being warriors and hunters. Families in the band needed them. They provided food and protection. The family was the most important part of Sioux life.

Children were the center of attention in Sioux families. At an early age, they learned what they had to do as members of the tribe. Men and women had different jobs. Men mostly hunted and went to war. They made tools and weapons. Women dried the meat after a hunt. They also tanned the skins. Women gathered roots, berries, and other plants to eat. They set up camp and made the meals. They also cared for the children and made the clothing.

▲ *Sioux men planning a raid*

▲ *A Sioux camp in about 1890*

When the Sioux began hunting on horseback, it changed things. Life became easier for the men and harder for the women.

On horseback, a good hunter might kill five buffalo in one day. It took a woman about three days to cut up and prepare one buffalo. To get the work done, good hunters often married more than one wife.

The Arrival of White Settlers

In the 1800s, white traders and settlers began traveling through Sioux land. They made roads through the hunting grounds and sacred places of the Sioux.

▲ *White settlers began moving west and staying in Sioux lands.*

One famous road was called the Oregon Trail. It led west to California.

In the 1850s, thousands of people traveled on the Oregon Trail to look for gold in California. Along the way, some settlers stayed in Sioux country. They built houses there and began to farm the land. Soon, fights broke out between the settlers and the Sioux.

▲ *Gold was a powerful draw and Easterners moved west.*

▲ *The Sioux signed several treaties with the government.*

The U.S. government tried to keep the settlers safe. They made an agreement, or peace **treaty**, with the Sioux and other Indian tribes. It was called the Fort Laramie Treaty of 1851.

The treaty said that the Sioux and other tribes had to live in certain areas. It promised that the settlers would stay out of these areas. This was the first of many treaties the United States made with the Sioux. And it was the first of many treaties it broke.

The Sioux Wars

▲ *The Sioux were forced to move west onto reservations.*

Between 1851 and 1859, the Dakota Sioux had to give up most of their land in Minnesota. U.S. soldiers moved them to **reservations**. Reservations were areas the U.S. government set aside for Indians to live on.

In return for taking the Indians' land, the government promised to pay the Sioux money. It also promised to give them food and other supplies. But the government did not keep these promises.

In the early 1860s, when the Civil War broke out in the United States, the government fell behind in giving food and money to the Sioux. Many Dakota were starving.

In August 1862, some Dakota broke into a government warehouse. They stole food to feed their families. Then a Dakota chief named Little Crow led more

▲ *Chief Little Crow*

attacks on trading posts and settlements in southern Minnesota.

▲ *Sioux outside a trading company in Nebraska*

The U.S. government ordered its troops to the area. The Dakota warriors fought back, but the soldiers were too strong. They killed many Dakota. They forced others to move to reservations in Nebraska. Some Dakota fled to Canada.

Fighting to Keep the Land

The Lakota Sioux were also fighting U.S. soldiers. They were trying to stop them from building a road to Bozeman, Montana. The Lakota did not want the road to cross their hunting grounds in the Bighorn Mountains. In 1865, a Sioux chief named Red

▲ *Chief Red Cloud*

Cloud led attacks to stop the road's construction.

For the next three years, Red Cloud and another Sioux chief named Crazy Horse continued the attacks. In 1868, the U.S. government gave up the fight. They signed the second Fort Laramie Treaty with the Indians.

▲ *The U.S. government signs the second Treaty of Fort Laramie.*

In this treaty, the U.S. government promised to give up the Bozeman Trail. The Sioux promised to stop their attacks and move to reservations.

Red Cloud and a leader named Spotted Tail agreed to live on a reservation. But Crazy Horse, Sitting Bull, and their people refused.

▲ *Bozeman, Montana, as it looks today*

The Little Bighorn

▲ *A reenactment of the Battle of Little Bighorn*

The second Fort Laramie Treaty did not last long. By the 1870s, both whites and American Indians had broken the treaty.

In the mid-1870s, gold was discovered in the Black Hills of South Dakota. Thousands of gold-seekers

▲ *Lieutenant Colonel George Armstrong Custer*

swarmed onto the Sioux reservation.

This situation set off another round of fighting. More U.S. troops were called in. Soon, all the Sioux were sent back to the reservation.

In June 1876, a large band of Sioux and Cheyenne were camped along the Little Bighorn River in

▲ *The battlefield where Custer and his troops met the Sioux warriors*

Montana. Lieutenant Colonel George Armstrong Custer and his troops attacked them. The Sioux fought back. Their leaders were Crazy Horse, Sitting Bull, and Gall.

The battle is now known as Custer's Last Stand. When it was over, Custer and every one of his troops were dead. But this was the last battle the Sioux would win.

In 1877, Crazy Horse and other Sioux chiefs entered the reservation. Crazy Horse was killed on September 5, 1877, when he would not let the soldiers take him to prison. Sitting Bull fled to Canada.

▲ *A monument marks the spot of the Battle of Little Bighorn.*

Wounded Knee Creek

Four years later, Sitting Bull and his followers came back to the United States. They gave themselves up to the U.S. Army. Sitting Bull was held prisoner for two years. Then he joined Buffalo Bill's Wild West show. The show toured Europe.

▲ *Chief Sitting Bull*

In 1890, some Lakota Sioux were following a new religion. It was called the Ghost Dance religion. Its followers believed that white people would leave all Native American lands. And Sioux warriors would be free to hunt the buffalo. It gave the Sioux people hope. Sitting Bull let the people of his camp practice this religion.

The U.S. government believed that the Ghost Dance religion was dangerous. They arrested its leaders. Many people in the government thought Sitting Bull would cause trouble. So, on December 15, 1890, they sent soldiers to arrest him. During the arrest, someone killed Sitting Bull.

▲ *Sitting Bull speaks to his followers.*

▲ *Wounded Knee*

Sitting Bull's death made his followers frightened and angry. Many ran away. They joined Big Foot's band near Pine Ridge, South Dakota. The soldiers followed them.

On December 28, 1890, the U.S. Army found Big Foot's band at Wounded Knee Creek. The Sioux surrendered to the soldiers. But in the morning, someone fired a gun. The soldiers began shooting. When it was over, more than 200 Lakota Sioux were dead.

It was a sad day at Wounded Knee Creek. The Sioux had lost their long battle to save their way of life. All their leaders were dead. And their spirits were broken.

▲ *A ridge overlooking Wounded Knee as it looks today*

The Sioux Today

After the **massacre** of Wounded Knee, the Sioux had to live as white Americans. For many years, they were not allowed to speak their own language. They could not follow their old traditions. Their children were taken away from them. They were sent to

▲ Sioux children were forced to go to boarding schools.

▲ *A U.S. school for Indian children at Pine Ridge, South Dakota*

boarding schools. There the children learned to speak and act as white Americans. In 1924, the Sioux became citizens of the United States.

▲ *Today, many Sioux live in South Dakota.*

In 1980, the U.S. Supreme Court ordered the government to pay the Sioux $105 million for the Indian land it took in 1877. The Sioux would not take the money. Instead, they asked the government to give back part of the Black Hills in South Dakota.

Today, more than 103,000 Sioux live in the United States and Canada. They are one of the largest Native American tribes in North America.

▲ *A teacher works with students on the Rosebud Reservation in South Dakota.*

▲ *Sioux friends*

Most Sioux live on reservations in Minnesota, Nebraska, North Dakota, South Dakota, and Montana. They work in casino, farming, and ranching jobs. Some even raise buffalo. Many have teaching and government jobs.

There are still many problems on Indian reservations today. But the Sioux are working hard to make their lives better. You can read about them in a newspaper published by the Pine Ridge Reservation in South Dakota. It is called *Indian Country Today*.

Glossary

bands—groups of people who live together

boarding schools—schools that provide meals and lodging

fasted—went without food

Great Plains—the big prairies in the western United States and Canada

massacre—the unnecessary killing of a large number of human beings

nation—an American Indian tribe or group of tribes under one government

nomads—people who move in groups in search of food

reservations—large areas of land set aside for Native Americans; in Canada reservations are called reserves

sacred—blessed

tan—to change animal skin into leather

treaty—an agreement between two governments

Woodland people—Native Americans who lived in the forests of the northeastern and southeastern United States

Did You Know?

- A single stone monument marks the gravesite where 250 Sioux were buried after the Wounded Knee Massacre of 1890. You can visit the site outside the community of Wounded Knee, South Dakota.

- A giant statue of Crazy Horse is being carved out of a mountain in South Dakota. You can visit it at the Crazy Horse Memorial, which is 17 miles (27 kilometers) southwest of Mount Rushmore.

- The Sioux have a sacred mountain in South Dakota called Mato paha, or Bear Butte. They hold religious ceremonies there today. You can visit the site in Bear Butte State Park, 6 miles (10 kilometers) northeast of Sturgis, South Dakota.

- Billy Mills, a Lakota Sioux, won the 10,000-meter race at the Olympic Games in Tokyo, Japan, in 1964.

At a Glance

Tribal name: Sioux

Divisions: Dakota, Nakota, Lakota

Past locations: Minnesota, Wisconsin, Wyoming, Montana, North Dakota, South Dakota, Nebraska

Present locations: Minnesota, Montana, North Dakota, South Dakota, Nebraska, and Canada

Traditional houses: Tepees

Traditional clothing material: Skins

Traditional transportation: Horses

Traditional food: Meat, wild plants

Important Dates

1851	The Dakota Sioux are forced to give up their Minnesota lands and move to reservations.
1862– 1864	The Sioux rebel in Minnesota and are defeated.
1866– 1868	Chief Red Cloud leads attacks to stop construction of the Bozeman Trail through Wyoming and Montana.
1868	The second Fort Laramie Treaty is signed.
1876	Battle of the Little Bighorn takes place.
1877	Chief Crazy Horse is shot dead after resisting imprisonment.
1881	Sitting Bull and his band surrender at Fort Buford, North Dakota.
1890	U.S. troops kill 250 Sioux at Wounded Knee Creek. The Sioux wars end.
1924	The Sioux become U.S. citizens.
1980	The U.S. Supreme Court orders the government to pay the Sioux $105 million for the land it took in 1877.

Want to Know More?

At the Library

Bruchac, Joseph. *A Boy Called Slow: The True Story of Sitting Bull.* New York: Philomel, 1996.

Landau, Elaine. *The Sioux.* New York: Franklin Watts, 1989.

Nicholson, Robert. *The Sioux.* New York: Chelsea Juniors, 1994.

On the Web

The Great Sioux Nation
http://www.travelsd.com
For information about Sioux history, tribal headquarters, landmarks, legends, and points of interest

Sioux Heritage
http://www.Lakhota.com
For extensive information about the Sioux language and culture and links to related sites

Through the Mail

Oglala Sioux Tribe Parks and Recreation Authority
P.O. Box 570
Kyle, SD 57752
To get information about visiting tribal parks and recreation sites

On the Road

The Heritage Center, Pine Ridge
Red Cloud Indian School
Pine Ridge, SD 57770
(North of Pine Ridge, on Highway 19)
605/867-1105
To see painting, graphics, and sculptures by current American Indian artists

Index

About the Author

Petra Press is a freelance writer of young adult nonfiction, specializing in the diverse culture of the Americas. Her more than twenty books include histories of U.S. immigration, education, and settlement of the West, as well as portraits of numerous indigenous cultures. She lives in with her husband, David, in Milwaukee, Wisconsin.